HERSHEY'S
CONTENTS

For additional recipes, visit HERSHEY'S
website at www.hersheys.com/cookbook

HERSHEY'S

WHIP SOMETHING UP
WITH HERSHEY'S

Enjoy baking this holiday season with Hershey's Holiday Collection. Your recipes will turn out perfect every time using our versatile line of baking ingredients that include:

Hershey's Cocoa: Classic, unsweetened, non-alkalized cocoa powder. Ideal for rich chocolate cakes, frostings, brownies, hot cocoa, and other desserts.

Hershey's Dutch Processed Cocoa: Unsweetened, alkalized cocoa powder with a dark reddish color and a unique, rich flavor for hot cocoa and special chocolate desserts.

Hershey's Semi-Sweet Chocolate Chips: Classic, deep, rich, semi-sweet chocolate.

Hershey's Milk Chocolate Chips: Creamy Hershey's milk chocolate.

Reese's Peanut Butter Chips: Reese's peanut butter taste in a chip.

Hershey's Mini Kisses™ Baking Pieces: The big taste of Hershey's Kisses Chocolates, but one-third the size. Unwrapped and ready to be poured into batter or used as a garnish. Available in both milk chocolate and semi-sweet.

Hershey's Semi-Sweet MiniChips™: A slightly smaller version of Hershey's Semi-Sweet Chocolate Chips with the same great taste. Ideal for muffins, cakes, and pies.

Skor English Toffee Bits: The toffee center of a Skor candy bar, broken into pieces. Perfect for baking and toppings.

Heath® Milk Chocolate Toffee Bits: Milk chocolate-coated English toffee bits.

Heath® Almond Toffee Bits: Tasty almond toffee bits that can be substituted for Skor English Toffee Bits in most recipes.

Hershey's Cinnamon Chips: The newest member of Hershey's Bake Shoppe® family, it's cinnamon like you've never seen before.

Hershey's Butterscotch Chips: Rich butterscotch flavor.

Hershey's Premier White Chips: Delicious vanilla taste.

Hershey's Mint Chocolate Chips: Semi-sweet chocolate and the fresh taste of mint provide a scrumptious combination for brownies, cookies and other special desserts.

Hershey's Raspberry Chips: If you love chocolate and raspberry, you'll love these raspberry-flavored, semi-sweet chocolate chips.

Hershey's Holiday Bits: The ultimate holiday baking ingredient, these bits of Hershey's semi-sweet chocolate are coated with red, green, and white candy coatings.

Hershey's Unsweetened Baking Chocolate and Hershey's Semi-Sweet Baking Chocolate: It's Hershey's chocolate specially formulated for baking and divided into convenient, one-ounce bars for your decadent chocolate desserts. Available in unsweetened and semi-sweet varieties.

Mounds® Coconut Flakes: Moist, delicious, tender, flaked coconut for baking and decorating.

With such a variety of baking ingredients to choose from, your holiday baking possibilities are endless. Now you can make this holiday season special with a delicious Hershey's dessert. To help you find the perfect holiday recipe, we've included a recipe and product index, beginning on page 94. Happy Baking!

BREADS AND MUFFINS

**A bevy of treats from the oven
bursting with holiday flavors**

CINNAMON CHIP FILLED CRESCENTS

Makes 16 crescents

2 cans (8 oz. each) refrigerated quick crescent dinner rolls
2 tablespoons butter or margarine, melted
$1^2/3$ cups (10-oz. pkg.) HERSHEY'S Cinnamon Chips, divided
Cinnamon Chips Drizzle (recipe follows)

1. Heat oven to 375°F. Unroll dough; separate into 16 triangles.

2. Spread melted butter on each triangle. Sprinkle 1 cup cinnamon chips evenly over triangles; gently press chips into dough. Roll from shortest side of triangle to opposite point. Place, point side down, on ungreased cookie sheet; curve into crescent shape.

3. Bake 8 to 10 minutes or until golden brown. Drizzle with Cinnamon Drizzle. Serve warm.

Cinnamon Chips Drizzle: Place remaining $2/3$ cup chips and $1^1/2$ teaspoons shortening (do not use butter, margarine, spread or oil) in small microwave-safe bowl. Microwave at HIGH (100%) 1 minute; stir until chips are melted and mixture is smooth.

CHIPPY BANANA BREAD

Makes 12 servings

$1/3$ cup butter or margarine, softened

$2/3$ cup sugar

2 eggs

2 tablespoons milk

$1^3/4$ cups all-purpose flour

$1^1/4$ teaspoons baking powder

$3/4$ teaspoon salt

$1/2$ teaspoon baking soda

1 cup mashed ripe banana

1 cup HERSHEY'S Semi-Sweet Chocolate Chips

1. Heat oven to 350°F. Lightly grease 8×4×2-inch loaf pan.

2. Beat butter and sugar in large bowl on medium speed of mixer until creamy. Add eggs, one at a time, beating well after each addition. Add milk; beat until blended.

3. Stir together flour, baking powder, salt and baking soda; add alternately with banana to butter mixture, beating until smooth after each addition. Gently fold in chocolate chips. Pour batter into prepared pan.

4. Bake 60 to 65 minutes or until wooden pick inserted near center comes out clean. Cool 10 minutes. Remove from pan to wire rack; cool completely. For easier slicing, wrap in foil and store overnight.

STREUSEL-TOPPED CINNAMON CHIP MUFFINS

Makes 12 to 14 muffins

1 egg
$^3/_4$ cup milk
$^1/_3$ cup vegetable oil
1$^3/_4$ cups all-purpose flour
$^1/_3$ cup sugar
3 teaspoons baking powder
$^1/_2$ teaspoon salt
1$^2/_3$ cups (10-oz. pkg.) HERSHEY'S Cinnamon Chips
Streusel Topping (recipe follows)

1. Heat oven to 400°F. Line muffin cups (2½ inches in diameter) with paper bake cups.

2. Beat egg in bowl. Stir in milk and oil. Combine flour, sugar, baking powder and salt; add to egg mixture, stirring just until dry ingredients are moistened. Gently stir in chips. Fill muffin cups ⅔ full with batter. Sprinkle Streusel Topping over top.

3. Bake 20 minutes or until golden. Cool in cups 5 minutes; remove. Serve warm.

Streusel Topping: Combine $^1/_4$ cup all-purpose flour, 2 tablespoons sugar and 2 tablespoons softened butter or margarine; mix with fork until crumbly.

FUDGEY PEANUT BUTTER CHIP MUFFINS

Makes 12 to 15 muffins

$^1/_2$ cup applesauce

$^1/_2$ cup quick-cooking rolled oats

$^1/_4$ cup ($^1/_2$ stick) butter or margarine, softened

$^1/_2$ cup granulated sugar

$^1/_2$ cup packed light brown sugar

1 egg

$^1/_2$ teaspoon vanilla extract

$^3/_4$ cup all-purpose flour

$^1/_4$ cup HERSHEY'S Dutch Processed Cocoa or HERSHEY'S Cocoa

$^1/_2$ teaspoon baking soda

$^1/_4$ teaspoon ground cinnamon (optional)

1 cup REESE'S Peanut Butter Chips

Powdered sugar (optional)

1. Heat oven to 350°F. Line muffin cups (2½ inches in diameter) with paper bake cups.

2. Stir together applesauce and oats in small bowl; set aside. In large bowl, beat butter, granulated sugar, brown sugar, egg and vanilla until well blended. Add applesauce mixture; blend well. Stir together flour, cocoa, baking soda and cinnamon, if desired. Add to butter mixture, blending well. Stir in peanut butter chips. Fill muffin cups ¾ full with batter.

3. Bake 22 to 26 minutes or until wooden pick inserted in center comes out almost clean. Cool slightly in pan on wire rack. Sprinkle muffin tops with powdered sugar, if desired. Serve warm.

VARIATION: Fudgey Chocolate Chip Muffins: Omit Peanut Butter Chips. Add 1 cup HERSHEY'S Semi-Sweet Chocolate Chips.

CHOCOLATE QUICKIE STICKIES

Makes 4 dozen small rolls

8 tablespoons (1 stick) butter or margarine, divided
³/₄ cup packed light brown sugar
4 tablespoons HERSHEY'S Cocoa, divided
5 teaspoons water
1 teaspoon vanilla extract
¹/₂ cup coarsely chopped nuts (optional)
2 cans (8 oz. each) refrigerated quick crescent dinner rolls
2 tablespoons granulated sugar

1. Heat oven to 350°F.

2. Melt 6 tablespoons butter in small saucepan over low heat; add brown sugar, 3 tablespoons cocoa and water. Cook over medium heat, stirring constantly, just until mixture comes to a boil. Remove from heat; stir in vanilla. Spoon about 1 teaspoonful chocolate mixture into each of 48 small muffin cups (1³/₄ inches in diameter). Sprinkle ½ teaspoon nuts, if desired, into each cup; set aside.

3. Unroll dough; separate into 8 rectangles; firmly press perforations to seal. Melt remaining 2 tablespoons butter; brush over rectangles. Stir together granulated sugar and remaining 1 tablespoon cocoa; sprinkle over all rectangles. Starting at longer side, roll up each rectangle; pinch seams to seal. Cut each roll into 6 equal pieces. Press each piece gently into prepared pans, cut-side down.

4. Bake 11 to 13 minutes or until light brown. Remove from oven; cool 30 seconds. Invert onto cookie sheet. Let stand 1 minute; remove pans. Serve warm or cool completely.

NOTE: Rolls can be baked in two 8-inch round baking pans. Heat oven to 350°F. Cook chocolate mixture as directed; place half in each pan. Prepare rolls as directed; place 24 pieces, cut side down, in each pan. Bake 20 to 22 minutes. Cool and remove from pans, as directed above.

CINNAMON CHIP DANISH

Makes about 12 servings

    6 oz. cream cheese, softened
    3 tablespoons sugar
    1 egg yolk
1²/₃ cups (10-oz. pkg.) HERSHEY'S Cinnamon Chips, divided *
   10 frozen yeast rolls, thawed and risen
      Vanilla Glaze (recipe follows)

1. Beat cream cheese, sugar and egg yolk until well blended. Set aside 3 tablespoons cinnamon chips for garnish. Stir remaining chips into cream cheese mixture.

2. Spray board or counter with nonstick cooking spray. Combine rolls and roll to an 18×12-inch rectangle. Spread filling over center-third (lengthwise portion) of rectangle. Cut 1-inch wide strips from edge of filling to edge of dough along 18-inch sides. Begin braid by folding top row toward filling. Alternately fold strips at an angle from each side across filling toward opposite side. Fold bottom row toward filling and finish by stretching last strip and tucking under.

3. Spray baking sheet with nonstick cooking spray. Support braid with both hands and place diagonally on baking sheet. Cover with sprayed plastic wrap; let rise 25 to 30 minutes. Heat oven to 350ºF. Bake 30 minutes or until golden brown. Cool; drizzle with Vanilla Glaze. Garnish with reserved chips.

Reese's Peanut Butter Chips or HERSHEY'S Semi-Sweet Chocolate Chips can be substituted for the cinnamon chips.

Vanilla Glaze: Stir together ¹/₂ cup powdered sugar, 1¹/₂ teaspoons softened butter and enough milk until of desired consistency.

STAR-OF-THE-EAST FRUIT BREAD

Makes 2 loaves

$^1/2$ cup (1 stick) butter or margarine, softened
1 cup sugar
2 eggs
1 teaspoon vanilla extract
2 cups all-purpose flour
1 teaspoon baking soda
$^1/4$ teaspoon salt
1 cup mashed ripe banana (about 3 medium)
$^1/2$ cup chopped maraschino cherries, well-drained
1 can (11 oz.) mandarin orange segments, well-drained
$^1/2$ cup chopped dates or Calimyrna figs
1 cup HERSHEY'S Semi-Sweet Chocolate Chips
Chocolate Drizzle (recipe follows)

1. Heat oven to 350°F. Grease two 8½×4½×2⅝-inch loaf pans.

2. Beat butter and sugar in large bowl until fluffy. Add eggs and vanilla; beat well. Stir together flour, baking soda and salt; add alternately with mashed banana to butter mixture, blending well. Stir in cherries, orange segments, dates and chocolate chips. Divide batter evenly between prepared pans.

3. Bake 40 to 50 minutes or until golden brown. Cool; remove from pans. Drizzle tops of loaves with Chocolate Drizzle. Store tightly wrapped.

Chocolate Drizzle: Combine $^1/2$ cup HERSHEY'S Semi-Sweet Chocolate Chips and 2 tablespoons whipping cream in small microwave-safe bowl. Microwave at HIGH (100%) 30 seconds; stir. If necessary, microwave at HIGH an additional 15 seconds; stir until chips are melted and mixture is smooth. Makes about $^1/2$ cup.

QUICK CINNAMON STICKY BUNS

Makes 12 cinnamon buns

  1 cup packed light brown sugar, divided
 10 tablespoons butter, softened and divided
  1 package (16-oz.) hot roll mix
  2 tablespoons granulated sugar
  1 cup hot water (120° to 130°F)
  1 egg
1²/₃ cups (10-oz. pkg.) HERSHEY'S Cinnamon Chips

1. Lightly grease two 9-inch round baking pans. Combine ½ cup brown sugar and 4 tablespoons softened butter in small bowl with pastry blender; sprinkle mixture evenly on bottom of prepared pans. Set aside.

2. Combine contents of hot roll mix package, including yeast packet, and granulated sugar in large bowl. Using spoon, stir in water, 2 tablespoons butter and egg until dough pulls away from sides of bowl. Turn dough onto lightly floured surface. With lightly floured hands, shape into ball. Knead 5 minutes or until smooth, using additional flour if necessary.

3. To shape: Using lightly floured rolling pin, roll into 15×12-inch rectangle. Spread with remaining 4 tablespoons butter. Sprinkle with remaining ½ cup brown sugar and cinnamon chips, pressing lightly into dough. Starting with 12-inch side, roll tightly as for jelly roll; seal edges.

4. Cut into 1-inch-wide slices with floured knife. Arrange 6 slices, cut sides down, in each prepared pan. Cover with towel; let rise in warm place until doubled, about 30 minutes.

5. Heat oven to 350°F. Uncover rolls. Bake 25 to 30 minutes or until golden brown. Cool 2 minutes in pan; with knife, loosen around edges of pan. Invert onto serving plates. Serve warm or at room temperature.

HERSHEY'S

BROWNIES AND BARS

When you want more than a cookie but not quite cake

PEANUTTY CRANBERRY BARS

Makes about 16 bars

$^1/_2$ cup (1 stick) butter or margarine, softened
$^1/_2$ cup granulated sugar
$^1/_4$ cup packed light brown sugar
  1 cup all-purpose flour
  1 cup quick-cooking rolled oats
$^1/_4$ teaspoon baking soda
$^1/_4$ teaspoon salt
  1 cup REESE'S Peanut Butter Chips
1$^1/_2$ cups fresh or frozen whole cranberries
$^2/_3$ cup light corn syrup
$^1/_2$ cup water
  1 teaspoon vanilla extract

1. Heat oven to 350°F. Grease 8-inch square baking pan.

2. Beat butter, granulated sugar and brown sugar in medium bowl until fluffy. Stir together flour, oats, baking soda and salt; gradually add to butter mixture, mixing until mixture is consistency of coarse crumbs. Stir in peanut butter chips.

3. Reserve 1½ cups mixture for crumb topping. Firmly press remaining mixture evenly into prepared pan. Bake 15 minutes or until set. Meanwhile, in medium saucepan, combine cranberries, corn syrup and water. Cook over medium heat, stirring occasionally, until mixture boils. Reduce heat; simmer 15 minutes, stirring occasionally. Remove from heat. Stir in vanilla. Spread evenly over baked layer. Sprinkle reserved 1½ cups crumbs evenly over top.

4. Return to oven. Bake 15 to 20 minutes or until set. Cool completely in pan on wire rack. Cut into bars.

WINTER WONDERLAND SNOWMEN BROWNIES

Makes about 12 large brownies or 36 squares

$^3/_4$ cup HERSHEY'S Cocoa or HERSHEY'S Dutch Processed Cocoa

$^1/_2$ teaspoon baking soda

$^2/_3$ cup butter or margarine, melted and divided

$^1/_2$ cup boiling water

2 cups sugar

2 eggs

1 teaspoon vanilla extract

1$^1/_2$ cups all-purpose flour

1$^2/_3$ cups (10-oz. pkg.) REESE'S Peanut Butter Chips

Powdered sugar (optional)

1. Heat oven to 350°F. Line 13×9×2-inch baking pan with foil; grease foil.

2. Stir together cocoa and baking soda in large bowl; stir in ⅓ cup melted butter. Add boiling water; stir until mixture thickens. Stir in sugar, eggs, vanilla and remaining ⅓ cup butter; stir until smooth. Add flour; stir until blended. Stir in peanut butter chips. Pour into prepared pan.

3. Bake 35 to 40 minutes or until brownies begin to pull away from sides of foil. Cool completely in pan. Cover; refrigerate until firm. Remove from pan; remove foil. Cut into snowmen shapes with cookie cutters or cut into squares. Just before serving, sprinkle with powdered sugar, if desired.

COCONUT BUTTERSCOTCH BARS

Makes 36 bars

$^1/_2$ cup (1 stick) butter or margarine, softened

$^1/_2$ cup powdered sugar

1 cup all-purpose flour

1 can (14 oz.) sweetened condensed milk (not evaporated milk)

1 cup HERSHEY'S Butterscotch Chips

$1^1/_3$ cups MOUNDS Coconut Flakes

1 teaspoon vanilla extract

1. Heat oven to 350°F.

2. Beat butter and powdered sugar in bowl until blended. Add flour; mix well. Pat mixture onto bottom of ungreased 9-inch square baking pan. Bake 12 to 15 minutes or until lightly browned. Combine sweetened condensed milk, butterscotch chips, coconut and vanilla; spread over baked layer.

3. Bake 25 to 30 minutes or until golden brown around edges. (Center will not appear set.) Cool completely in pan on wire rack. Cut into bars.

CREAMY FILLED BROWNIES
Makes about 24 brownies

1/2 cup (1 stick) butter or margarine
1/3 cup HERSHEY'S Cocoa
2 eggs
1 cup sugar
1/2 cup all-purpose flour
1/4 teaspoon baking powder
1/4 teaspoon salt
1 teaspoon vanilla extract
1 cup finely chopped nuts
Creamy Filling (recipe follows)
MiniChip Glaze (recipe follows)
1/2 cup sliced almonds or chopped nuts (optional)

1. Heat oven to 350°F. Line 15½×10½×1-inch jelly roll pan with foil; grease foil.

2. Melt butter in small saucepan; remove from heat. Stir in cocoa until smooth. Beat eggs in medium bowl; gradually add sugar, beating until fluffy. Stir together flour, baking powder and salt; add to egg mixture. Add cocoa mixture and vanilla; beat well. Stir in nuts. Spread batter into prepared pan.

3. Bake 12 to 14 minutes or until top springs back when touched lightly in center. Cool completely in pan on wire rack; remove from pan to cutting board. Remove foil; cut brownie in half crosswise. Spread one half with Creamy Filling; top with second half. Spread Mini Chip Glaze over top; sprinkle with almonds, if desired. After glaze has set, cut into bars.

Mini Chip Glaze: Heat 1/4 cup sugar and 2 tablespoons water to boiling in small saucepan. Remove from heat. Immediately add 1/2 cup HERSHEY'S MINICHIPS Semi-Sweet Chocolate, stirring until melted.

Creamy Filling: Beat 1 package (3 oz.) softened cream cheese, 2 tablespoons softened butter or margarine and 1 teaspoon vanilla extract in small bowl. Gradually add 1½ cups powdered sugar, beating until of spreading consistency.

FILLING VARIATIONS:
Coffee: Add 1 teaspoon powdered instant coffee.
Orange: Add 1/2 teaspoon freshly grated orange peel and 1 or 2 drops orange food color.
Almond: Add 1/4 teaspoon almond extract.

CHOCOLATE FUDGE PECAN PIE BARS

Makes about 36 bars

$2^2/_3$ cups all-purpose flour

$1^1/_4$ cups packed light brown sugar, divided

1 cup (2 sticks) cold butter or margarine

4 eggs

1 cup light corn syrup

4 bars (1 oz. each) HERSHEY'S Unsweetened Baking Chocolate, unwrapped and melted

2 teaspoons vanilla extract

$^1/_2$ teaspoon salt

2 cups coarsely chopped pecans

1. Heat oven to 350°F. Grease 15½×10½×1-inch jelly-roll pan.

2. Stir together flour and ¼ cup brown sugar in large bowl. With pastry blender, cut in butter until mixture resembles coarse crumbs; press onto bottom of prepared pan.

3. Bake 10 to 15 minutes or until set. Remove from oven. With back of spoon, lightly press crust into corners and against sides of pan.

4. Beat eggs, corn syrup, remaining 1 cup brown sugar, melted chocolate, vanilla and salt; stir in pecans. Pour mixture evenly over warm crust. Return to oven.

5. Bake 25 to 30 minutes or until chocolate filling is set. Cool completely in pan on wire rack. Cut into bars.

HERSHEY'S BEST BROWNIES

Makes about 36 brownies

1 cup (2 sticks) butter or margarine

2 cups sugar

2 teaspoons vanilla extract

4 eggs

$3/4$ cup HERSHEY'S Cocoa or HERSHEY'S Dutch Processed Cocoa

1 cup all-purpose flour

$1/2$ teaspoon baking powder

$1/4$ teaspoon salt

1 cup chopped nuts (optional)

1. Heat oven to 350°F. Grease 13×9×2-inch baking pan.

2. Place butter in large microwave-safe bowl. Microwave at HIGH (100%) 2 to 2½ minutes or until melted. Stir in sugar and vanilla. Add eggs, one at a time, beating well with spoon after each addition. Add cocoa; beat until well blended. Add flour, baking powder and salt; beat well. Stir in nuts, if desired. Pour batter into prepared pan.

3. Bake 30 to 35 minutes or until brownies begin to pull away from sides of pan. Cool completely in pan on wire rack. Cut into bars.

HOLIDAY RED RASPBERRY CHOCOLATE BARS

Makes 36 bars

2$^1/_2$ cups all-purpose flour

1 cup sugar

$^3/_4$ cup finely chopped pecans

1 cup (2 sticks) cold butter or margarine

1 egg, beaten

1 jar (12 oz.) seedless red raspberry jam

1$^2/_3$ cups HERSHEY'S Milk Chocolate Chips, HERSHEY'S Semi-Sweet Chocolate Chips, HERSHEY'S Raspberry Chips, or HERSHEY'S MINI KISSES Milk Chocolate Baking Pieces

1. Heat oven to 350°F. Grease 13×9×2-inch baking pan.

2. Stir together flour, sugar, pecans, butter and egg in large bowl. Cut in butter with pastry blender or fork until mixture resembles coarse crumbs; set aside 1½ cups crumb mixture. Press remaining crumb mixture on bottom of prepared pan; spread jam over top. Sprinkle with chocolate chips. Crumble remaining crumb mixture evenly over top.

3. Bake 40 to 45 minutes or until lightly browned. Cool completely in pan on wire rack; cut into bars.

HERSHEY'S

CRANBERRY ORANGE RICOTTA CHEESE BROWNIES

Makes about 16 brownies

- $1/2$ cup (1 stick) butter or margarine, melted
- $3/4$ cup sugar
- 1 teaspoon vanilla extract
- 2 eggs
- $3/4$ cup all-purpose flour
- $1/2$ cup HERSHEY'S Cocoa
- $1/2$ teaspoon baking powder
- $1/2$ teaspoon salt
- Cheese Filling (recipe follows)

1. Heat oven to 350°F. Grease 9-inch square baking pan.

2. Stir together butter, sugar and vanilla in medium bowl; add eggs, beating well. Stir together flour, cocoa, baking powder and salt; add to butter mixture, mixing thoroughly. Spread half of chocolate batter in prepared pan. Spread Cheese Filling over top. Drop remaining chocolate batter by teaspoonfuls onto cheese filling.

3. Bake 40 to 45 minutes or until wooden pick inserted in center comes out clean. Cool completely in pan on wire rack. Cut into squares. Refrigerate leftover brownies

CHEESE FILLING

- 1 cup ricotta cheese
- $1/4$ cup sugar
- 3 tablespoons whole-berry cranberry sauce
- 2 tablespoons cornstarch
- 1 egg
- $1/4$ to $1/2$ teaspoon freshly grated orange peel
- 4 drops red food color (optional)

Beat ricotta cheese, sugar, cranberry sauce, cornstarch and egg in small bowl until smooth. Stir in orange peel and food color, if desired.

TOFFEE-TOPPED FUDGEY BROWNIES

Makes about 36 brownies

$1^1/4$ cups ($2^1/2$ sticks) butter or margarine

2 cups sugar

2 teaspoons vanilla extract

4 eggs

$1^1/2$ cups all-purpose flour

$3/4$ cup HERSHEY'S Cocoa

$1^3/4$ cups (10-oz. pkg.) HEATH Almond Toffee Bits

$3/4$ cup HERSHEY'S MINICHIPS Chocolate

1. Heat oven to 350°F. Grease 13×9×2-inch baking pan.

2. Melt butter in medium saucepan over low heat. Remove from heat; stir in sugar and vanilla. Add eggs, one at a time, beating just until blended.

3. Combine flour and cocoa; gradually add to butter mixture, stirring just until blended. (Do not overmix.) Spread batter into prepared pan. Sprinkle with toffee bits and chocolate chips.

4. Bake 35 minutes or until wooden pick inserted in center comes out clean. Cool completely in pan on wire rack. Cut into squares.

CHOCOLATE CHIP CANDY COOKIE BARS

Makes about 48 bars

$1^2/_3$ cups all-purpose flour

2 tablespoons plus $1^1/_2$ cups sugar, divided

$3/_4$ teaspoon baking powder

1 cup (2 sticks) cold butter or margarine, divided

1 egg, slightly beaten

$1/_2$ cup plus 2 tablespoons (5-oz. can) evaporated milk, divided

2 cups (12-oz. pkg.) HERSHEY'S Semi-Sweet Chocolate Chips, divided

$1/_2$ cup light corn syrup

$1^1/_2$ cups sliced almonds

1. Heat oven to 375°F.

2. Stir together flour, 2 tablespoons sugar and baking powder in medium bowl; using pastry blender, cut in ½ cup butter until mixture forms coarse crumbs. Stir in egg and 2 tablespoons evaporated milk; stir until mixture holds together in ball shape. Press onto bottom and ¼-inch up sides of 15½×10½×1-inch jelly-roll pan.

3. Bake 8 to 10 minutes or until lightly browned; remove from oven, leaving oven on. Sprinkle 1½ cups chocolate chips evenly over crust; do not disturb chips.

4. Place remaining 1½ cups sugar, remaining ½ cup butter, remaining ½ cup evaporated milk and corn syrup in 3-quart saucepan. Cook over medium heat, stirring constantly, until mixture boils; stir in almonds. Continue cooking and stirring to 240°F on candy thermometer (soft-ball stage) or until small amount of mixture, when dropped into very cold water, forms a soft ball which flattens when removed from water. (Bulb of candy thermometer should not rest on bottom of saucepan.) Remove from heat. Immediately spoon almond mixture evenly over chips and crust; do not spread.

5. Bake 10 to 15 minutes or just until almond mixture is golden brown. Remove from oven; cool 5 minutes. Sprinkle remaining ½ cup chips over top; cool completely. Cut into bars.

CHEERY CHEESECAKE COOKIE BARS

Makes 36 bars

4 bars (1 oz. each) HERSHEY'S Unsweetened Baking Chocolate, broken into pieces

1 cup (2 sticks) butter

2^1/$_2$ cups sugar, divided

4 eggs

1 teaspoon vanilla extract

2 cups all-purpose flour

1 package (8 oz.) cream cheese, softened

1^3/$_4$ cups (10-oz. pkg.) HERSHEY'S MINI KISSES Milk Chocolate or Semi-Sweet Baking Pieces, divided

^{1}/$_2$ cup chopped red or green maraschino cherries

^{1}/$_2$ teaspoon almond extract

Few drops red food color (optional)

1. Heat oven to 350°F. Grease 13×9×2-inch baking pan.

2. Place baking chocolate and butter in large microwave-safe bowl. Microwave at HIGH (100%) 2 to 2½ minutes, stirring after each minute, until mixture is melted. Beat in 2 cups sugar, 3 eggs and vanilla until blended. Stir in flour; spread batter into prepared pan.

3. Beat cream cheese, remaining ½ cup sugar and remaining 1 egg; stir in 1¼ cups baking pieces, cherries, almond extract and red food color, if desired. Drop by spoonfuls over top of chocolate mixture in pan.

4. Bake 35 to 40 minutes or just until set. Remove from oven; immediately sprinkle remaining ½ cup baking pieces over top. Cool completely in pan on wire rack; cut into bars. Cover; refrigerate leftover bars.

CAKES AND CHEESECAKES

Ultra-decadent creations for every holiday gathering

REFRESHING CHOCO-ORANGE CHEESECAKE

Makes 12 servings

- 1 cup graham cracker crumbs
- $1/4$ cup ($1/2$ stick) butter or margarine, melted
- 2 cups sugar, divided
- 1 cup HERSHEY'S Semi-Sweet Chocolate Chips
- 3 packages (8 oz. each) cream cheese, softened
- 4 eggs
- $1^1/2$ cups dairy sour cream
- 2 teaspoons orange extract
- 1 teaspoon freshly grated orange peel
- Whipped topping

1. Stir together graham cracker crumbs, melted butter and ¼ cup sugar in small bowl; pat firmly onto bottom of 9-inch springform pan.

2. Place chocolate chips in medium microwave-safe bowl. Microwave at HIGH (100%) 1 minute or just until chips are melted when stirred.

3. Beat cream cheese and remaining 1¾ cups sugar in large bowl; add eggs, one at a time, beating after each addition. Stir in sour cream and orange extract. Stir 3 cups cream cheese mixture into melted chocolate chips; pour into crust. Freeze 10 to 15 minutes or until chocolate sets.

4. Heat oven to 325°F. Stir orange peel into remaining cream cheese mixture; gently spread over chocolate mixture.

5. Bake 1 hour 15 minutes or until set except for 3-inch circle in center; turn off oven. Let stand in oven, with door ajar, 1 hour; remove from oven. With knife, loosen cheesecake from side of pan. Cool completely; remove side of pan. Cover; refrigerate. Garnish with whipped topping and orange wedges, if desired. Cover; refrigerate leftover cheesecake.

FRENCH YULE LOG

Makes 10 to 12 servings

 Powdered sugar

 4 eggs, separated

 $^3/_4$ cup sugar, divided

 $^3/_4$ cup ground blanched almonds

 $^1/_3$ cup all-purpose flour

 $^1/_3$ cup HERSHEY'S Cocoa

 $^1/_2$ teaspoon baking soda

 $^1/_4$ teaspoon salt

 $^1/_4$ cup water

 1 teaspoon vanilla extract

 $^1/_4$ teaspoon almond extract

 Whipped Cream Filling (recipe follows)

 Creamy Cocoa Log Frosting (recipe follows)

1. Heat oven to 375°F. Line 15×10½-inch jelly-roll pan with foil; generously grease foil. Sift powdered sugar onto clean towel.

2. Beat egg yolks in medium bowl 3 minutes on medium speed of mixer. Gradually add ½ cup sugar, beating another 2 minutes until thick and lemon-colored. Combine almonds, flour, cocoa, baking soda and salt; add alternately with water to egg yolk mixture, beating on low speed just until blended. Stir in vanilla and almond extracts.

3. Beat egg whites in large bowl until foamy. Gradually add ¼ cup sugar, beating until stiff peaks form. Carefully fold chocolate mixture into beaten egg whites. Spread batter evenly into prepared pan.

4. Bake 16 to 18 minutes or until top springs back when lightly touched. Cool in pan on wire rack 10 minutes; remove from pan onto prepared towel. Carefully remove foil. Cool completely.

5. Cut into four equal rectangles approximately 3½×10 inches. Chill layers while preparing filling and frosting. Place one cake layer on serving plate. Spread one-third (about 1 cup) Whipped Cream Filling evenly over cake layer; top with another cake layer. Repeat with remaining cake and filling, ending with cake layer. Refrigerate about 1 hour before frosting. Generously frost loaf with Creamy Cocoa Log

Frosting. Swirl frosting with spatula or score with fork to resemble bark. Refrigerate at least 4 hours before serving. Garnish with shaved chocolate and holly, if desired. Cover; refrigerate leftover dessert.

WHIPPED CREAM FILLING

Makes about 3 cups filling

$1^1/_2$ cups cold whipping cream
$^1/_3$ cup powdered sugar
1 teaspoon vanilla extract

Combine whipping cream, powdered sugar and vanilla in large bowl. Beat until cream is stiff. (Do not overbeat.)

CREAMY COCOA FROSTING

Makes 2 $^1/_2$ cups frosting

$3^1/_2$ cups powdered sugar
$^1/_2$ cup HERSHEY'S Cocoa
$^1/_2$ cup (1 stick) butter or margarine, softened
2 tablespoons light corn syrup
2 teaspoons vanilla extract
$^1/_3$ cup milk

Combine powdered sugar and cocoa. Beat butter, ½ cup cocoa mixture, corn syrup and vanilla in medium bowl until smooth. Add remaining cocoa mixture alternately with milk, beating until smooth and of spreading consistency.

ULTRA CHOCOLATE CHEESECAKE

Makes 12 servings

Mocha Crumb Crust (recipe follows)
3 packages (8 oz. each) cream cheese, softened
1 1/4 cups sugar
1 container (8 oz.) dairy sour cream
2 teaspoons vanilla extract
1/2 cup HERSHEY'S Cocoa
2 tablespoons all-purpose flour
3 eggs
Chocolate Drizzle (recipe follows)

1. Prepare Mocha Crumb Crust. Heat oven to 350°F.

2. Beat cream cheese and sugar in large bowl until fluffy. Add sour cream and vanilla; beat until blended. Add cocoa and flour; beat until blended. Add eggs; beat well. Pour into crust.

3. Bake 50 to 55 minutes or until set. Remove from oven to wire rack. With knife, loosen cake from side of pan. Cool completely; remove side of pan. Prepare Chocolate Drizzle; drizzle over top. Refrigerate 4 to 6 hours. Cover; refrigerate leftover cheesecake.

MOCHA CRUMB CRUST

1 1/4 cups vanilla wafer crumbs
1/4 cup sugar
1/4 cup HERSHEY'S Cocoa
1 teaspoon powdered instant espresso or coffee
1/3 cup butter, melted

Heat oven to 350°F. In medium bowl, stir together crumbs, sugar, cocoa and instant espresso. Add butter; stir until well blended. Press mixture firmly onto bottom and 1-inch up side of 9-inch springform pan. Bake 8 minutes; cool slightly.

Chocolate Drizzle: Place 1/2 cup HERSHEY'S Semi-Sweet Chocolate Chips and 2 teaspoons shortening (do not use butter, margarine or oil) in small microwave-safe bowl. Microwave at HIGH (100%) 30 seconds; stir. If necessary, microwave at HIGH an additional 15 seconds at a time, stirring after each heating, just until chips are melted and mixture is smooth.

EASY COCOA CAKE

Makes 12 to 15 servings

1 cup (2 sticks) butter or margarine
1 cup water
$^1/_4$ cup HERSHEY'S Cocoa
2 cups all-purpose flour
2 cups sugar
1 teaspoon baking soda
$^1/_2$ teaspoon salt
2 eggs
$^1/_2$ cup dairy sour cream
Cocoa Fudge Frosting (recipe follows)

1. Heat oven to 350°F. Grease and flour 13×9×2-inch baking pan.

2. Combine butter, water and cocoa in small saucepan. Cook over medium heat, stirring constantly, until mixture boils; remove from heat. Stir together flour, sugar, baking soda and salt in large bowl. Stir in hot cocoa mixture. Add eggs and sour cream; beat on medium speed of mixer until well blended. Pour batter into prepared pan.

3. Bake 30 to 35 minutes or until wooden pick inserted in center comes out clean. While cake is still hot, frost with Cocoa Fudge Frosting. Cool completely in pan on wire rack.

COCOA FUDGE FROSTING

Makes about 1 cup frosting

$^1/_4$ cup ($^1/_2$ stick) butter or margarine
$^1/_4$ cup milk
2 tablespoons HERSHEY'S Cocoa
Dash salt
$^1/_2$ teaspoon vanilla extract
2 cups powdered sugar

1. Combine butter, milk, cocoa and salt in small saucepan. Cook over medium heat, stirring constantly, until mixture is smooth and slightly thickened. Remove from heat; stir in vanilla.

2. Place powdered sugar in medium bowl; add cocoa mixture. Beat just until smooth. Use immediately.

HOLIDAY FUDGE TORTE

Makes 8 to 10 servings

  1 cup all-purpose flour
 $^3/_4$ cup sugar
 $^1/_4$ cup HERSHEY'S Cocoa
1$^1/_2$ teaspoons powdered instant coffee
 $^3/_4$ teaspoon baking soda
 $^1/_4$ teaspoon salt
 $^1/_2$ cup (1 stick) butter or margarine, softened
 $^3/_4$ cup dairy sour cream
  1 egg
 $^1/_2$ teaspoon vanilla extract
    Fudge Nut Glaze (recipe follows)

1. Heat oven to 350°F. Grease 9-inch round baking pan; line bottom with wax paper. Grease paper; flour paper and pan.

2. Stir together flour, sugar, cocoa, instant coffee, baking soda and salt in large bowl. Add butter, sour cream, egg and vanilla; beat on low speed of mixer until blended. Increase speed to medium; beat 3 minutes. Pour batter into prepared pan.

3. Bake 30 to 35 minutes or until wooden pick inserted in center comes out clean. Cool 10 minutes. Remove from pan to wire rack; gently peel off wax paper. Cool completely.

4. Prepare Fudge Nut Glaze. Place cake on serving plate; pour glaze evenly over cake, allowing some to run down sides. Refrigerate until glaze is firm, about 1 hour. Cover; refrigerate leftover torte.

FUDGE NUT GLAZE

 $^1/_2$ cup whipping cream
 $^1/_4$ cup sugar
  1 tablespoon butter
1$^1/_2$ teaspoons light corn syrup
 $^1/_3$ cup HERSHEY'S Semi-Sweet Chocolate Chips
 $^3/_4$ cup hazelnuts, macadamia nuts or pecans
 $^1/_2$ teaspoon vanilla extract

1. Combine all ingredients except nuts and vanilla in small saucepan. Cook over medium heat, stirring constantly, until mixture boils. Cook, stirring constantly, 5 minutes. Remove from heat.

2. Cool 10 minutes; stir in nuts and vanilla.

VIENNESE CHOCOLATE TORTE

Makes 10 servings

$^1/_4$ cup HERSHEY'S Cocoa

$^1/_4$ cup boiling water

$^1/_3$ cup shortening

$^3/_4$ cup sugar

$^1/_2$ teaspoon vanilla extract

1 egg

1 cup all-purpose flour

$^3/_4$ teaspoon baking soda

$^1/_4$ teaspoon salt

$^2/_3$ cup buttermilk or sour milk*

$^1/_4$ cup seedless black raspberry preserves

Cream Filling (recipe follows)

Cocoa Glaze (recipe follows)

MOUNDS Coconut Flakes, toasted

1. Heat oven to 350°F. Lightly grease 15½×10½×1-inch jelly-roll pan; line pan with wax paper and lightly grease paper.

2. Stir together cocoa and boiling water in small bowl until smooth; set aside. Beat shortening, sugar and vanilla in medium bowl until creamy; beat in egg. Stir together flour, baking soda and salt; add alternately with buttermilk to shortening mixture. Add reserved cocoa mixture, beating just until blended. Spread batter into pan.

3. Bake 16 to 18 minutes or until wooden pick inserted in center comes out clean. Cool 10 minutes; remove from pan. Remove wax paper; cool completely. Cut cake crosswise into three equal pieces. Place one piece on serving plate; spread 2 tablespoons preserves evenly on top of cake. Spread half of Cream Filling over preserves. Repeat layering. Glaze top of torte with Cocoa Glaze, allowing some to drizzle down sides. Garnish with coconut. Refrigerate several hours. Cover; refrigerate leftover torte.

* To sour milk: Use 2 teaspoons white vinegar plus milk to equal $^2/_3$ cup.

Cream Filling: Beat 1 cup whipping cream, 2 tablespoons powdered sugar and 1 teaspoon vanilla extract in small bowl until stiff. Makes about 2 cups filling.

COCOA GLAZE

- 2 tablespoons butter or margarine
- 2 tablespoons HERSHEY'S Cocoa
- 2 tablespoons water
- 1 cup powdered sugar
- 1/2 teaspoon vanilla extract

Melt butter in saucepan. Stir in cocoa and water. Cook, stirring constantly, until mixture thickens. Do NOT boil. Remove from heat. Whisk in powdered sugar gradually. Add vanilla and beat with whisk until smooth. Add additional water ½ teaspoon at a time until desired consistency.

HOLIDAY CHOCOLATE CAKE

Makes 10 to 12 servings

2 cups sugar

1³/₄ cups all-purpose flour

³/₄ cup HERSHEY'S Cocoa

2 teaspoons baking soda

1 teaspoon baking powder

1 teaspoon salt

2 eggs

1 cup buttermilk or sour milk*

1 cup strong black coffee or 2 teaspoons instant coffee dissolved in 1 cup hot water

¹/₂ cup vegetable oil

2 teaspoons vanilla extract

Ricotta Cheese Filling (recipe follows)

Chocolate Whipped Cream (recipe follows)

Vanilla Whipped Cream (recipe follows)

1. Heat oven to 350°F. Grease and flour two 9-inch round baking pans.

2. Stir together sugar, flour, cocoa, baking soda, baking powder and salt in large bowl. Add eggs, buttermilk, coffee, oil and vanilla; beat at medium speed of mixer 2 minutes (batter will be thin). Pour batter into prepared pans.

3. Bake 30 to 35 minutes or until wooden pick inserted in center of cake comes out clean. Cool 10 minutes; remove from pans to wire racks. Cool completely.

4. Slice cake layers in half horizontally. Place bottom slice on serving plate; top with ⅓ Ricotta Cheese Filling. Alternate cake layers and filling, ending with cake on top. Frost cake with Chocolate Whipped Cream. Decorate with Vanilla Whipped Cream and cherries, if desired. Cover; refrigerate leftover cake.

* To sour milk: Use 1 tablespoon white vinegar plus milk to equal 1 cup.

RICOTTA CHEESE FILLING

1³/₄ cups (15 oz.) ricotta cheese*

¹/₄ cup sugar

3 tablespoons Grand Marnier (orange-flavored liqueur) or orange juice concentrate, undiluted

$^1/_4$ cup candied red or green cherries, coarsely chopped
$^1/_3$ cup HERSHEY'S MINICHIPS Semi-Sweet Chocolate

Beat ricotta cheese, sugar and liqueur in large bowl until smooth. Fold in candied cherries and small chocolate chips.

1 cup ($^1/_2$ pt.) whipping cream may be substituted for ricotta cheese. Beat with sugar and liqueur until stiff. Fold in candied cherries and small chocolate chips.

Chocolate Whipped Cream: Stir together $^1/_3$ cup powdered sugar and 2 tablespoons HERSHEY'S Cocoa in small bowl. Add 1 cup ($^1/_2$ pt.) cold whipping cream and 1 teaspoon vanilla extract; beat until stiff.

Vanilla Whipped Cream: Beat $^1/_2$ cup cold whipping cream, 2 tablespoons powdered sugar and $^1/_2$ teaspoon vanilla extract in small bowl until stiff.

CHOCOLATE & FRUIT CAKE FOR KWANZAA

Makes 10 to 12 servings

$^3/_4$ cup HERSHEY'S Cocoa

1$^3/_4$ cups sugar, divided

$^1/_2$ cup water

$^1/_4$ cup shortening

$^1/_2$ cup (1 stick) butter or margarine, softened

1 teaspoon vanilla extract

3 eggs

1$^1/_3$ cups all-purpose flour

1 teaspoon baking soda

1 teaspoon salt

$^2/_3$ cup milk

Citrus Filling (recipe follows)

4 cups fresh fruit (sliced peaches or nectarines; strawberries; blueberries; kiwifruit; sweet cherries, halved)

$^1/_2$ cup green grapes, halved

1. Heat oven to 350°F. Grease and flour two 9-inch round baking pans.

2. Stir together cocoa, ½ cup sugar, water and shortening in small saucepan. Cook over low heat, stirring constantly, until shortening is melted and sugar is dissolved. Remove from heat; cool.

3. Beat butter, remaining 1¼ cups sugar and vanilla in large bowl until creamy. Add eggs, one at a time, beating well after each addition. Add cocoa mixture, beating until blended. Stir together flour, baking soda and salt; add alternately with milk to butter mixture. Pour batter into prepared pans.

4. Bake 35 to 40 minutes or until wooden pick inserted in center comes out clean. Cool 10 minutes; remove from pans to wire racks. Cool completely.

5. Prepare Citrus Filling. With a long serrated knife, using a sawing motion, split each cake layer in half horizontally, forming 4 layers. Place 1 layer on serving plate; spread about ⅓ cup filling over layer. Top with about 1 cup assorted fruit. Top with second cake layer; repeat procedure until all layers are stacked. Arrange fruit on top layer in a decorative design. Top with remaining filling, if desired. Garnish with grapes. Refrigerate until serving time. Cover; refrigerate leftover cake.

CITRUS FILLING

Makes about 1²/₃ cups filling

- 1 cup sugar
- 3 tablespoons cornstarch
- ¹/₄ teaspoon salt
- 1 cup orange juice
- ¹/₄ cup lemon juice
- ¹/₄ cup water
- 1 tablespoon butter or margarine
- 1 teaspoon freshly grated orange peel
- ¹/₂ teaspoon freshly grated lemon peel

Combine sugar, cornstarch, salt, orange juice, lemon juice and water in small saucepan. Cook over medium heat, stirring constantly, until mixture boils; boil and stir 1 minute. Remove from heat; stir in butter, orange and lemon peel. Refrigerate until cool.

DECADENT HOLIDAY CHOCOLATE TORTE

Makes 12 servings

3 eggs, separated
$1/8$ teaspoon cream of tartar
$1^1/2$ cups sugar
1 cup (2 sticks) butter or margarine, melted
2 teaspoons vanilla extract
$1/2$ cup all-purpose flour
$1/2$ cup HERSHEY'S Cocoa or HERSHEY'S Dutch Processed Cocoa
$1/4$ cup water
1 cup finely chopped pecans
Semi-Sweet Glaze (recipe follows)
Snowy White Cut-Outs (optional)
HERSHEY'S Holiday Bits (optional)

1. Heat oven to 350°F. Line bottom and sides of 9-inch springform pan with foil; grease foil.

2. Beat egg whites and cream of tartar in small bowl until soft peaks form; set aside. Beat egg yolks, sugar, melted butter and vanilla in large bowl until well blended. Add flour, cocoa and water; stir in pecans. Gradually fold reserved egg white mixture into chocolate mixture; spread into prepared pan.

3. Bake 45 to 55 minutes or until firm to touch; cool completely in pan on wire rack. Invert onto serving plate; remove foil. Cover; refrigerate. Prepare Semi-Sweet Glaze. Spread top and sides of torte with prepared glaze. Cover; refrigerate. Prepare Snowy White Cut-Outs, if desired; garnish top of torte with cut-outs. Press holiday bits onto sides, if desired.

Semi-Sweet Glaze: Place 1 cup HERSHEY'S Semi-Sweet Chips and $1/3$ cup whipping cream in small microwave-safe bowl. Microwave at HIGH (100%) 1 minute; stir until smooth. Use immediately.

Snowy White Cut-Outs: Line tray with heavy duty foil. Melt $1^2/3$ cups (10-oz. pkg.) HERSHEY'S Premier White Chips and 1 teaspoon shortening (do not use butter, margarine, spread or oil) as directed on package. Immediately spread mixture about $1/8$-inch thick on prepared tray. Before mixture is firm, cut into desired shapes with small cookie cutters; do not remove from tray. Cover; refrigerate until firm. Gently peel off shapes.

CHOCOLATE SPICE CAKE

Makes 12 to 15 servings

$1^3/4$ cups all-purpose flour

$1^1/4$ cups sugar

$1/3$ cup HERSHEY'S Cocoa

2 teaspoons baking soda

1 teaspoon ground cinnamon

$1/2$ teaspoon ground nutmeg

$1/4$ teaspoon ground allspice

$1/8$ teaspoon salt

$1^1/2$ cups applesauce

$1/2$ cup milk

$1/2$ cup (1 stick) butter or margarine, melted

1 teaspoon vanilla extract

1 cup chopped nuts (optional)

$1/2$ cup raisins

Vanilla Glaze (recipe follows)

1. Heat oven to 350°F. Grease and flour 13×9×2-inch baking pan.

2. Stir together flour, sugar, cocoa, baking soda, cinnamon, nutmeg, allspice and salt in large bowl. Stir in applesauce, milk, butter and vanilla; beat until well blended. Add nuts, if desired, and raisins. Pour batter into prepared pan.

3. Bake 40 to 45 minutes or until wooden pick inserted in center comes out clean. Cool completely in pan on wire rack. Drizzle with Vanilla Glaze.

Vanilla Glaze: Combine $1^1/4$ cups powdered sugar, 2 tablespoons softened butter or margarine, 1 to 2 tablespoons hot water or milk and $1/2$ teaspoon vanilla extract in medium bowl; beat with whisk until smooth and of desired consistency. Makes about $3/4$ cup glaze.

HERSHEY'S

CANDY

**Classy confections that make great gifts
(even to yourself)**

FESTIVE FUDGE
Makes about 2 pounds

3 cups (1^1/$_2$ pkgs., 12 oz. each) HERSHEY'S Semi-Sweet
  Chocolate Chips
1 can (14 oz.) sweetened condensed milk (not evaporated
  milk)
  Dash salt
^{1}/$_2$ to 1 cup chopped nuts (optional)
1^1/$_2$ teaspoons vanilla extract

1. Line 8- or 9-inch square pan with wax paper.

**2. Melt chocolate chips with sweetened condensed milk
and salt in heavy saucepan over low heat. Remove from
heat; stir in nuts, if desired, and vanilla. Spread evenly into
prepared pan.**

**3. Refrigerate 2 hours or until firm. Turn fudge onto
cutting board; peel off paper and cut into squares. Store
covered in refrigerator.**

**VARIATION: Chocolate Peanut Butter Chip Glazed Fudge
(pictured at right):** Proceed as above; stir in ^{2}/$_3$ cup REESE'S
Peanut Butter Chips in place of nuts. Melt 1 cup REESE'S
Peanut Butter Chips with ^{1}/$_2$ cup whipping cream; stir until
thick and smooth. Spread over fudge.

CHOCOLATE CHERRY COCONUT FUDGE

Makes about 36 pieces

2 cups sugar

$^1/_2$ cup HERSHEY'S Cocoa

1 cup milk

1 tablespoon light corn syrup

1 cup candied green and/or red cherries, chopped

$^1/_2$ cup MOUNDS Coconut Flakes

$^1/_3$ cup butter or margarine

1 teaspoon vanilla extract

$^1/_4$ teaspoon almond extract

Additional chopped candied green and/or red cherries and flaked coconut (optional)

1. Line 8-inch square pan with foil, extending foil over edges of pan.

2. Stir together sugar, cocoa, milk and corn syrup in medium saucepan. Cook over medium heat, stirring constantly, until mixture comes to full boil. Boil, without stirring, until mixture reaches 234°F on candy thermometer or until a small amount of syrup, when dropped into very cold water, forms a soft ball that flattens when removed from water. (Bulb of candy thermometer should not rest on bottom of saucepan.) Remove from heat. Do not stir. Cool at room temperature 25 minutes.

3. Add cherries, coconut, butter, vanilla and almond extracts. Beat with wooden spoon until fudge thickens and loses some of its gloss. (This will take less than 5 minutes). Quickly spread into prepared pan. If desired, sprinkle additional candied cherries and coconut over top. Cool at room temperature until firm.

4. Using foil, lift fudge out of pan; place on cutting board. Peel off foil. Cut into squares. Store, covered at room temperature.

NOTE: For best results, do not double this recipe.

PEANUT BUTTER CHIP BRITTLE

Makes about 2 pounds brittle

1²/₃ cups (10-oz. pkg.) REESE'S Peanut Butter Chips, divided
1¹/₂ cups (3 sticks) butter or margarine
1³/₄ cups sugar
   3 tablespoons light corn syrup
   3 tablespoons water

1. Butter 15½×10½×1-inch jelly-roll pan.* Sprinkle 1 cup peanut butter chips evenly onto bottom of prepared pan; set aside.

2. Melt butter in heavy 2½-quart saucepan; stir in sugar, corn syrup and water. Cook over medium heat, stirring constantly, until mixture reaches 300°F on candy thermometer. (This should take 30 to 35 minutes. Bulb of thermometer should not rest on bottom of saucepan.)

3. Remove from heat. Immediately spread mixture into prepared pan; sprinkle with remaining ⅔ cup peanut butter chips. Cool completely. Remove from pan. Break into pieces. Store in tightly covered container in cool, dry place.

* For thicker brittle, use a 13×9-inch pan.

CHOCOLATE BUTTERCREAM CHERRY CANDIES

Makes about 48 candies

About 48 maraschino cherries with stems, well drained
$^1/_4$ cup ($^1/_2$ stick) butter, softened
2 cups powdered sugar
$^1/_4$ cup HERSHEY'S Cocoa or HERSHEY'S Dutch Processed Cocoa
1 to 2 tablespoons milk, divided
$^1/_2$ teaspoon vanilla extract
$^1/_4$ teaspoon almond extract
White Chip Coating (recipe follows)
Chocolate Chip Drizzle (recipe follows)

1. Cover tray with wax paper. Lightly press cherries between layers of paper towels to remove excess moisture.

2. Beat butter, powdered sugar, cocoa and 1 tablespoon milk in small bowl until well blended; stir in vanilla and almond extract. If necessary, add remaining milk, one teaspoon at a time, until mixture will hold together but is not wet.

3. Mold scant teaspoon mixture around each cherry, covering completely; place on prepared tray. Cover; refrigerate 3 hours or until firm.

4. Prepare White Chip Coating. Holding each cherry by stem, dip into coating. Place on tray; refrigerate until firm.

5. About 1 hour before serving, prepare Chocolate Chip Drizzle; with tines of fork, drizzle randomly over candies. Refrigerate until drizzle is firm. Store in refrigerator.

White Chip Coating: Place $1^2/_3$ cups (10-oz. pkg.) HERSHEY'S Premier White Chips in small microwave-safe bowl; drizzle with 2 tablespoons vegetable oil. Microwave at HIGH (100%) 1 minute; stir. If necessary, microwave at HIGH an additional 15 seconds at a time, stirring after each heating just until chips are melted and mixture is smooth. If mixture thickens while coating, microwave at HIGH 15 seconds; stir until smooth.

Chocolate Chip Drizzle: Place $^1/_4$ cup HERSHEY'S Semi-Sweet Chocolate Chips and $^1/_4$ teaspoon shortening (do not use butter, margarine, spread or oil) in another small microwave-safe bowl. Microwave at HIGH (100%) 30 seconds to 1 minute; stir until chips are melted and mixture is smooth.

MOCHA TRUFFLES

Makes about 16 truffles
(pictured on page 81)

$^1/_4$ cup whipping cream

3 tablespoons sugar

3 tablespoons butter

$1^1/_2$ teaspoons powdered instant coffee

$^1/_2$ cup HERSHEY'S Semi-Sweet Chocolate Chips

$^1/_2$ teaspoon vanilla extract

  Chopped nuts or HERSHEY'S Semi-Sweet Baking
  Chocolate, grated

1. Combine whipping cream, sugar, butter and instant coffee in small saucepan. Cook over low heat, stirring constantly, just until mixture boils.

2. Remove from heat; immediately add chocolate chips. Stir until chips are melted and mixture is smooth when stirred; add vanilla. Pour into small bowl; refrigerate, stirring occasionally, until mixture begins to set. Cover; refrigerate several hours or overnight to allow mixture to ripen and harden.

3. Shape small amounts of mixture into 1-inch balls, working quickly to prevent melting; roll in nuts or chocolate. Cover; store in refrigerator. Serve cold.

CHOCOLATE PEANUT CLUSTERS

Makes about 2 dozen candies

$^1/_2$ cup HERSHEY'S Milk Chocolate Chips
$^1/_2$ cup HERSHEY'S Semi-Sweet Chocolate Chips
  1 tablespoon shortening (do not use butter, margarine, spread or oil)
  1 cup unsalted, roasted peanuts OR raisins

1. Place milk chocolate chips, semi-sweet chocolate chips and shortening in small microwave-safe bowl. Microwave at HIGH (100%) 1 to 1½ minutes or just until chips are melted and mixture is smooth when stirred. Stir in peanuts.

2. Drop by teaspoons into 1-inch diameter candy or petit four papers. Refrigerate until firm, about 30 minutes. Store in tightly covered container in refrigerator.

JINGLE BELLS CHOCOLATE PRETZELS

Makes 24 coated pretzels

1 cup HERSHEY'S Semi-Sweet Chocolate Chips

1 cup HERSHEY'S Premier White Chips, divided

1 tablespoon plus $^1/_2$ teaspoon shortening (do not use butter, margarine, spread or oil), divided

About 24 salted or unsalted pretzels (3×2 inches)

1. Cover tray or cookie sheet with wax paper.

2. Place chocolate chips, ⅔ cup white chips and 1 tablespoon shortening in medium microwave-safe bowl. Microwave at HIGH (100%)1 minute; stir. Microwave at HIGH an additional 1 to 2 minutes, stirring every 30 seconds, until chips are melted when stirred.

3. Using fork, dip each pretzel into chocolate mixture; tap fork on side of bowl to remove excess chocolate. Place coated pretzels on prepared tray.

4. Place remaining ⅓ cup white chips and remaining ½ teaspoon shortening in small microwave-safe bowl. Microwave at HIGH 15 to 30 seconds or until chips are melted when stirred. Using tines of fork, drizzle chip mixture across pretzels. Refrigerate until coating is set. Store in airtight container in cool, dry place.

VARIATION: White Dipped Pretzels: Cover tray with wax paper. Place 1$^2/_3$ cups (10-oz. pkg.) HERSHEY'S Premier White Chips and 2 tablespoons shortening (do not use butter, margarine, spread or oil) in medium microwave-safe bowl. Microwave at HIGH 1 to 2 minutes or until chips are melted when stirred. Dip pretzels as directed above. Place $^1/_4$ cup HERSHEY'S Semi-Sweet Chocolate Chips and $^1/_4$ teaspoon shortening (do not use butter, margarine, spread or oil) in small microwave-safe bowl. Microwave at HIGH 30 seconds to 1 minute or until chips are melted when stirred. Drizzle melted chocolate across pretzels, using tines of fork. Refrigerate and store as directed above.

RICH COCOA FUDGE

Makes about 36 pieces or 1³/₄ pounds

  3 cups sugar
²/₃ cup HERSHEY'S Cocoa or HERSHEY'S Dutch Processed Cocoa
¹/₈ teaspoon salt
1¹/₂ cups milk
¹/₄ cup (¹/₂ stick) butter
  1 teaspoon vanilla extract

1. Line 8- or 9-inch square pan with foil, extending foil over edges of pan. Butter foil.

2. Mix sugar, cocoa and salt in heavy 4-quart saucepan; stir in milk. Cook over medium heat, stirring constantly, until mixture comes to full rolling boil. Boil, without stirring, until mixture reaches 234°F on candy thermometer or until small amount of mixture dropped into very cold water forms a soft ball which flattens when removed from water. (Bulb of candy thermometer should not rest on bottom of saucepan.)

3. Remove from heat. Add butter and vanilla. DO NOT STIR. Cool at room temperature to 110°F (lukewarm). Beat with wooden spoon until fudge thickens and just begins to lose some of its gloss. Quickly spread into prepared pan; cool completely. Cut into squares. Store in tightly covered container at room temperature.

VARIATIONS: Nutty Rich Cocoa Fudge: Beat cooked fudge as directed. Immediately stir in 1 cup chopped almonds, pecans or walnuts and spread quickly into prepared pan.

Marshmallow-Nut Cocoa Fudge: Increase cocoa to ³/₄ cup. Cook fudge as directed. Add 1 cup marshmallow creme with butter and vanilla. DO NOT STIR. Cool to 110°F (lukewarm). Beat 8 minutes; stir in 1 cup chopped nuts. Pour into prepared pan. (Fudge does not set until poured into pan.)

NOTE: For best results, do not double this recipe.

QUICK HOLIDAY RASPBERRY FUDGE

Makes about 48 pieces

$3^1/_3$ cups (two 10-oz. pkgs.) HERSHEY'S Raspberry Chips OR $3^1/_3$ cups HERSHEY'S Semi-Sweet Chocolate Chips

1 can (14 oz.) sweetened condensed milk (not evaporated milk)

$1^1/_2$ teaspoons vanilla extract or raspberry-flavored liqueur

1. Line 8-inch square pan with foil, extending foil over edges of pan.

2. Place raspberry chips and sweetened condensed milk in medium microwave-safe bowl. Microwave at HIGH (100%) 1 minute; stir. If necessary, microwave an additional 30 seconds at a time, stirring after each heating until chips are melted and mixture is smooth; stir in vanilla. Spread evenly into prepared pan.

3. Cover; refrigerate 2 hours or until firm. Remove from pan; place on cutting board. Peel off foil; cut into squares. Store loosely covered at room temperature.

NOTE: For best results, do not double this recipe.

HERSHEY'S

COOKIES

**These morsels of goodness continue
to be the most popular holiday treat**

OATMEAL TOFFEE COOKIES

Makes about 4 dozen cookies

1 cup (2 sticks) butter or margarine, softened

2 eggs

2 cups packed light brown sugar

2 teaspoons vanilla extract

1 $^3/_4$ cups all-purpose flour

1 teaspoon baking soda

1 teaspoon ground cinnamon

$^1/_2$ teaspoon salt

3 cups quick-cooking oats

1 $^3/_4$ cups (10-oz. pkg.) HEATH Almond Toffee Bits OR SKOR English Toffee Bits

1 cup MOUNDS Coconut Flakes (optional)

1. Heat oven to 375°F. Lightly grease cookie sheet. Beat butter, eggs, brown sugar and vanilla until well blended. Add flour, baking soda, cinnamon and salt; beat until blended.

2. Stir in oats, toffee and coconut, if desired, with spoon. Drop dough by rounded teaspoons about 2 inches apart onto prepared sheet.

3. Bake 8 to 10 minutes or until edges are lightly browned. Cool 1 minute; remove to wire rack.

DOUBLE PEANUT BUTTER COOKIES

Makes about 4 dozen cookies

$^1/_4$ cup ($^1/_2$ stick) butter or margarine, softened

$^1/_4$ cup shortening

$^1/_2$ cup REESE'S Creamy Peanut Butter

$^1/_2$ cup granulated sugar

$^1/_2$ cup packed light brown sugar

1 egg

$1^1/_4$ cups all-purpose flour

$^3/_4$ teaspoon baking soda

$^1/_2$ teaspoon baking powder

$^1/_4$ teaspoon salt

$1^2/_3$ cups (10-oz. pkg.) REESE'S Peanut Butter Chips

1. Heat oven to 375°F.

2. Combine butter, shortening, peanut butter, granulated sugar, brown sugar and egg in large bowl; beat on medium speed of mixer until well blended. Stir together flour, baking soda, baking powder and salt; gradually add to butter mixture, beating until blended. Stir in peanut butter chips.

3. Shape dough into 1-inch balls. Place 2 inches apart onto ungreased cookie sheet. Using a fork dipped in additional granulated sugar, flatten balls to about ¼-inch thickness by pressing fork in two directions to form a crisscross pattern.

4. Bake 8 to 10 minutes or until set. Cool slightly; remove from cookie sheet to wire rack. Cool completely.

REESE'S CHEWY CHOCOLATE COOKIES

Makes about 4½ dozen cookies

  2 cups all-purpose flour
$^3/_4$ cup HERSHEY'S Cocoa
  1 teaspoon baking soda
$^1/_2$ teaspoon salt
$1^1/_4$ cups ($2^1/_2$ sticks) butter or margarine, softened
  2 cups sugar
  2 eggs
  2 teaspoons vanilla extract
$1^2/_3$ cups (10-oz. pkg.) REESE'S Peanut Butter Chips

1. Heat oven to 350°F. Stir together flour, cocoa, baking soda and salt; set aside.

2. Beat butter and sugar in large bowl with mixer until fluffy. Add eggs and vanilla; beat well. Gradually add flour mixture, beating well. Stir in peanut butter chips. Drop by rounded teaspoons onto ungreased cookie sheet.

3. Bake 8 to 9 minutes. (Do not overbake; cookies will be soft. They will puff while baking and flatten while cooling.) Cool slightly; remove from cookie sheet to wire rack. Cool completely.

HOLIDAY DOUBLE CHOCOLATE COOKIES

Makes about 3½ dozen cookies

1½ cups all-purpose flour

½ cup HERSHEY'S Cocoa

½ teaspoon baking soda

¼ teaspoon salt

½ cup (1 stick) butter or margarine, softened

¾ cup packed light brown sugar

½ cup granulated sugar

1 teaspoon vanilla extract

2 eggs

1⅓ cups (10-oz. pkg.) HERSHEY'S Holiday Bits, divided

1. Heat oven to 350°F. Lightly grease cookie sheet.

2. Stir together flour, cocoa, baking soda and salt. In large bowl, beat butter, brown sugar, granulated sugar and vanilla until well blended. Add eggs; beat well. Gradually add flour mixture, blending well. Stir in 1 cup Holiday Bits. Drop by rounded teaspoons onto prepared cookie sheet. Press 8 to 9 of remaining bits on dough before baking.

3. Bake 7 to 9 minutes or until cookie is set. Do not overbake. Cool slightly; remove from cookie sheet to wire rack. Cool completely.

CHEWY CHOCOLATE-CINNAMON COOKIES

Makes about 40 cookies

6 tablespoons butter or margarine, softened
$^2/_3$ cup packed light brown sugar
3 tablespoons plus $^1/_4$ cup granulated sugar, divided
1 egg
1 teaspoon baking soda
$^1/_2$ cup light corn syrup
1 teaspoon vanilla extract
$1^1/_2$ cups all-purpose flour
$^1/_3$ cup HERSHEY'S Cocoa
$^1/_4$ to $^1/_2$ teaspoon ground cinnamon

1. Heat oven to 350°F. Spray cookie sheet with nonstick cooking spray.

2. Beat butter until creamy. Add brown sugar and 3 tablespoons granulated sugar; beat until blended. Add egg, baking soda, corn syrup and vanilla; beat well.

3. Stir together flour and cocoa; beat into butter mixture. If batter becomes too stiff, use wooden spoon to stir in remaining flour. Cover; refrigerate about 30 minutes, if necessary, until batter is firm enough to shape. Shape dough into 1-inch balls. Combine ¼ cup granulated sugar and cinnamon; roll balls in mixture. Place balls 2 inches apart on prepared cookie sheet.

4. Bake 9 to 10 minutes or until cookies are set and tops are cracked. Cool slightly; remove from cookie sheet to wire rack. Cool completely.

CHOCOLATE SNOWBALL COOKIES

Makes about 4 dozen cookies

1 cup (2 sticks) butter or margarine, softened
$3/4$ cup packed light brown sugar
1 egg
1 teaspoon vanilla extract
2 cups all-purpose flour
$1/2$ cup HERSHEY'S Dutch Processed Cocoa or HERSHEY'S Cocoa
1 teaspoon baking powder
$1/4$ teaspoon baking soda
3 tablespoons milk
$3/4$ cup finely chopped macadamia nuts or almonds
$3/4$ cup SKOR English Toffee Bits
Powdered sugar

1. Beat butter, brown sugar, egg and vanilla in large bowl until blended. Stir together flour, cocoa, baking powder and baking soda; add with milk to butter mixture until well blended. Stir in nuts and toffee.

2. Refrigerate until firm enough to handle, at least 2 hours. Heat oven to 350°F. Shape dough into 1-inch balls; place 2 inches apart on ungreased cookie sheet.

3. Bake 8 to 10 minutes or until set. Remove from cookie sheet to wire rack. Cool completely; roll in powdered sugar.

SENSATIONAL CINNAMON CHIP BISCOTTI

Makes about 5 dozen cookies

$^1/_2$ cup (1 stick) butter, softened

1 cup sugar

2 eggs

1 teaspoon vanilla extract

$2^1/_2$ cups all-purpose flour

$1^1/_2$ teaspoons baking powder

$^1/_4$ teaspoon salt

$1^2/_3$ cups (10-oz. pkg.) HERSHEY'S Cinnamon Chips (divided)

1 cup very finely chopped walnuts

2 teaspoons shortening (do not use butter, margarine, spread or oil)

White Chip Drizzle (recipe follows)

1. Heat oven to 325°F. Lightly grease cookie sheet.

2. Beat butter and sugar in large bowl until blended. Add eggs and vanilla; beat well. Stir together flour, baking powder and salt; gradually add to butter mixture, beating until smooth. (Dough will be stiff.) Using spoon or with hands, work 1 cup cinnamon chips and walnuts into dough.

3. Divide dough into four equal parts. Shape each part into a log about 8 inches long. Place on prepared cookie sheet, at least 2 inches apart; flatten slightly.

4. Bake 25 to 30 minutes or until logs are set and wooden pick inserted in center comes out clean. Remove from oven; let cool on cookie sheet 30 minutes. Transfer to cutting board. Using serrated knife and sawing motion, cut logs diagonally into ½-inch wide slices. Place slices close together, cut side down on ungreased cookie sheet. Return to oven; bake 5 to 6 minutes. Turn each slice; bake an additional 5 to 8 minutes. Remove from oven; cool slightly. Remove from cookie sheet to wire rack. Cool completely. Melt remaining cinnamon chips with shortening; drizzle over each cookie. Drizzle White Chip Drizzle over top.

White Chip Drizzle: Place $^1/_4$ cup HERSHEY'S Premier White Chips and 1 teaspoon shortening (do not use butter, margarine, spread or oil) in small microwave-safe bowl. Microwave at HIGH (100%) 30 to 45 seconds or until smooth when stirred.

CHOCOLATE-PEANUT BUTTER CHECKERBOARDS

Makes about 4½ dozen cookies

$^1/_2$ cup (1 stick) butter or margarine, softened
1 cup sugar
1 egg
1 teaspoon vanilla extract
1 cup plus 3 tablespoons all-purpose flour, divided
$^1/_2$ teaspoon baking soda
$^1/_4$ cup HERSHEY'S Cocoa
$^1/_2$ cup REESE'S Peanut Butter Chips, melted

1. Beat butter, sugar, egg and vanilla in large bowl until fluffy. Add 1 cup flour and baking soda; beat until blended. Remove ¾ cup batter to small bowl; set aside. Add cocoa and remaining 3 tablespoons flour to remaining batter in large bowl; blend well.

2. Place peanut butter chips in small microwave-safe bowl. Microwave at HIGH (100%) 30 seconds or until melted and smooth when stirred. Immediately add to batter in small bowl, stirring until smooth. Divide chocolate dough into four equal parts. Roll each part between plastic wrap or wax paper into a log 7 inches long and about 1 inch in diameter. Repeat with peanut butter dough. Wrap the eight rolls individually in wax paper or plastic wrap. Refrigerate several hours until very firm.

3. Heat oven to 350°F. Remove rolls from wax paper. Place 1 chocolate roll and 1 peanut butter roll side by side on a cutting board. Top each roll with another roll of the opposite flavor to make checkerboard pattern. Lightly push rolls together; repeat with remaining four rolls. Working with one checkerboard at a time (keep remaining checkerboard covered and refrigerated), cut into ¼-inch slices. Place on ungreased cookie sheet.

4. Bake 8 to 9 minutes or until peanut butter portion is lightly browned. Cool 1 minute; remove from cookie sheet to wire rack. Cool completely.

HOLIDAY MINI KISSES TREASURE COOKIES

Makes about 3 dozen cookies

1$^1/_2$ cups graham cracker crumbs

$^1/_2$ cup all-purpose flour

2 teaspoons baking powder

1 can (14 oz.) sweetened condensed milk (not evaporated milk)

$^1/_2$ cup (1 stick) butter, softened

1$^1/_3$ cups MOUNDS Coconut Flakes

1 cup HERSHEY'S MINI KISSES Milk Chocolate or Semi-Sweet Baking Pieces

1$^1/_3$ cups (10-oz. pkg.) HERSHEY'S Holiday Bits

1. Heat oven to 375°F. Stir together graham cracker crumbs, flour and baking powder in small bowl; set aside.

2. Beat sweetened condensed milk and butter until smooth; add reserved crumb mixture, mixing well. Stir in coconut, baking pieces and Holiday Bits. Drop by rounded tablespoons onto ungreased cookie sheet.

3. Bake 8 to 10 minutes or until lightly browned. Cool 1 minute; remove from cookie sheet to wire rack. Cool completely.

VARIATION: Use 1$^3/_4$ cups (10-oz. pkg.) HERSHEY'S MINI KISSES Milk Chocolate or Semi-Sweet Baking Pieces and 1 cup coarsely chopped walnuts. Omit Holiday Bits. Proceed as directed above.

HERSHEY'S DOUBLE CHOCOLATE MINT COOKIES

Makes about 2½ dozen cookies

²/₃ cup butter or margarine, softened

1 cup sugar

1 egg

1 teaspoon vanilla extract

1 cup all-purpose flour

¹/₂ cup HERSHEY'S Cocoa

¹/₂ teaspoon baking soda

¹/₄ teaspoon salt

1²/₃ cups (10-oz. pkg.) HERSHEY'S Mint Chocolate Chips

1. Heat oven to 350°F.

2. Beat butter and sugar in large bowl until creamy. Add egg and vanilla; beat well. Stir together flour, cocoa, baking soda and salt; gradually add to butter mixture, beating well. Stir in mint chocolate chips. Drop by rounded teaspoons onto ungreased cookie sheet.

3. Bake 8 to 9 minutes or just until set; do not overbake. Cool slightly; remove from cookie sheet to wire rack. Cool completely.

WHITE CHIP APRICOT OATMEAL COOKIES

Makes about 3½ dozen cookies

$3/4$ cup (1$1/2$ sticks) butter or margarine, softened
$1/2$ cup granulated sugar
$1/2$ cup packed light brown sugar
  1 egg
  1 cup all-purpose flour
  1 teaspoon baking soda
2$1/2$ cups rolled oats
1$2/3$ cups (10-oz. pkg.) HERSHEY'S Premier White Chips
 $3/4$ cup chopped dried apricots

1. Heat oven to 375°F.

2. Beat butter, granulated sugar and brown sugar in large bowl until fluffy. Add egg; beat well. Add flour and baking soda; beat until well blended. Stir in oats, white chips and apricots. Loosely form rounded teaspoons of batter into balls; place on ungreased cookie sheet.

3. Bake 7 to 9 minutes or just until lightly browned; do not overbake. Cool slightly; remove from cookie sheet to wire rack. Cool completely.

DESSERTS
AND PIES

Extraordinary endings for your holiday meals

SAUCY BRICKLE
ICE CREAM PIE

Makes 6 to 8 servings

About 35 vanilla wafer cookies

About $^1/_2$ gallon vanilla ice cream, slightly softened

$1^3/_4$ cups (10-oz. pkg.) HEATH Almond Toffee Bits OR SKOR English Toffee Bits, divided

1 cup sugar

$^3/_4$ cup light cream or evaporated milk

$^1/_4$ cup ($^1/_2$ stick) butter or margarine

$^1/_4$ cup light corn syrup

1. Butter bottom and sides of 9-inch pie plate; line with vanilla wafers. Spoon half of ice cream into prepared pie plate. Sprinkle ¾ cup toffee bits over ice cream. Spoon in remaining ice cream. Cover; freeze until firm, 4 to 6 hours.

2. Prepare sauce by combining sugar, light cream, butter and corn syrup in medium saucepan. Cook over low heat, stirring constantly, until mixture boils; boil and stir 1 minute. Remove from heat; stir in remaining 1 cup toffee bits. Cool, stirring occasionally (sauce will thicken as it cools).

3. Serve wedges of pie with sauce. Cover; store leftover pie in freezer. Cover; store leftover sauce in refrigerator.

Brickle Ice Cream Sundaes: Place scoops of ice cream in individual dessert dishes; spoon toffee sauce over top. Garnish with whipped topping and toffee bits.

WHITE & CHOCOLATE
COVERED STRAWBERRIES

Makes 2 to 3 dozen berries

$1^2/_3$ cups (10-oz. pkg.) HERSHEY'S Premier White Chips

2 tablespoons shortening (do not use butter, margarine, spread or oil)

1 cup HERSHEY'S Semi-Sweet Chocolate Chips

4 cups (2 pt.) fresh strawberries, rinsed, patted dry and chilled

1. Cover tray with wax paper.

2. Place white chips and 1 tablespoon shortening in medium microwave-safe bowl. Microwave at HIGH (100%) 1 minute; stir until chips are melted and mixture is smooth. If necessary, microwave at HIGH an additional 30 seconds at a time, just until smooth when stirred.

3. Holding by top, dip ⅔ of each strawberry into white chip mixture; shake gently to remove excess. Place on prepared tray; refrigerate until coating is firm, at least 30 minutes.

4. Repeat microwave procedure with chocolate chips in clean microwave-safe bowl. Dip lower ⅓ of each berry into chocolate mixture. Refrigerate until firm. Cover; refrigerate leftover strawberries.

White & Chocolate Covered Strawberries (this page)
and Mocha Truffles (recipe on page 56)

CHOCOLATE CHEESEPIE

Makes 8 servings

  1 cup graham cracker crumbs
1$^1/_2$ cups sugar, divided
  $^1/_4$ cup ($^1/_2$ stick) butter or margarine, melted
  2 bars (1 oz. each) HERSHEY'S Unsweetened Baking Chocolate, broken into pieces
  4 packages (3 oz. each) cream cheese, softened
    Dash salt
  1 teaspoon vanilla extract, divided
  3 eggs
  1 container (8 oz.) dairy sour cream
  $^1/_3$ cup sugar

1. Stir together crumbs, ¼ cup sugar and butter in small bowl. Press mixture firmly onto bottom and up side of 9-inch pie plate. Refrigerate 8 to 10 minutes.

2. Heat oven to 375°F. Place chocolate in small microwave-safe bowl. Microwave at HIGH (100%) 30 seconds; stir. Microwave an additional 10 to 20 second intervals, stirring after each heating until melted.

3. Beat cream cheese in medium bowl until fluffy; gradually beat in 1¼ cups sugar, salt and ½ teaspoon vanilla. Add melted chocolate; beat until well blended. Add eggs, one at a time, beating well after each addition. Pour into prepared crust.

4. Bake 20 minutes or until center is almost set. Remove from oven; cool 1 hour.

5. Stir together sour cream, remaining ½ teaspoon vanilla and ⅓ cup sugar. Spread evenly over top of pie. Bake at 375°F for 10 minutes. Cool to room temperature. Refrigerate until firm. Cover; refrigerate leftover pie.

EASY PEANUT BUTTER CHIP PIE
Makes 6 to 8 servings

1 package (3 oz.) cream cheese, softened
1 teaspoon lemon juice
1²/₃ cups (10-oz. pkg.) REESE'S Peanut Butter Chips, divided
²/₃ cup sweetened condensed milk (not evaporated milk)
1 cup (¹/₂ pt.) cold whipping cream, divided
1 packaged (6 oz.) chocolate or graham cracker crumb crust
1 tablespoon powdered sugar
1 teaspoon vanilla extract

1. Beat cream cheese and lemon juice in medium bowl on medium speed of mixer until fluffy, about 2 minutes; set aside.

2. Place 1 cup peanut butter chips and sweetened condensed milk in medium microwave-safe bowl. Microwave at HIGH (100%) 45 seconds; stir. If necessary, microwave an additional 15 seconds at a time, stirring after each heating, until chips are melted and mixture is smooth when stirred.

3. Add warm peanut butter mixture to cream cheese mixture. Beat on medium speed until blended, about 1 minute. Beat ½ cup whipping cream in small bowl until stiff; fold into peanut butter mixture. Pour into crust. Cover; refrigerate about 6 hours or until firm.

4. Just before serving, combine remaining ½ cup whipping cream, powdered sugar and vanilla in small bowl. Beat until stiff; spread over filling. Garnish with remaining peanut butter chips. Cover; refrigerate leftover pie.

PEANUT BUTTER AND CHOCOLATE MOUSSE PIE

Makes 6 to 8 servings

9-inch pie crust, baked and cooled

$1^2/_3$ cups (10-oz. pkg.) REESE'S Peanut Butter Chips, divided

1 package (3 oz.) cream cheese, softened

$^1/_4$ cup powdered sugar

$^1/_3$ cup plus 2 tablespoons milk

1 teaspoon unflavored gelatin

1 tablespoon cold water

2 tablespoons boiling water

$^1/_2$ cup sugar

$^1/_3$ cup HERSHEY'S Cocoa

1 cup ($^1/_2$ pt.) cold whipping cream

1 teaspoon vanilla extract

1. Melt 1½ cups peanut butter chips. Beat cream cheese, powdered sugar and ⅓ cup milk in medium bowl until smooth. Add melted chips; beat well. Beat in remaining 2 tablespoons milk. Spread into cooled crust.

2. Sprinkle gelatin over cold water in small bowl; let stand 1 minute to soften. Add boiling water; stir until gelatin is completely dissolved. Cool slightly. Combine sugar and cocoa in medium bowl; add whipping cream and vanilla. Beat on medium speed of mixer until stiff; pour in gelatin mixture, beating until well blended. Spoon into crust over peanut butter layer. Refrigerate several hours. Garnish with remaining chips. Cover; refrigerate leftover pie.

EASY FUDGE POTS DE CRÈME

Makes 8 servings

1 package (4-serving size) chocolate cook & serve pudding and pie
   filling mix*
2 cups half-and-half or whole milk
1 cup HERSHEY'S Semi-Sweet Chocolate Chips
   Sweetened whipped cream
   HERSHEY'S Cocoa

1. Stir together pudding mix and half-and-half in medium saucepan. Cook over medium heat, stirring constantly, until mixture comes to a full boil. Remove from heat.

2. Add chocolate chips; stir until chips are melted and mixture is smooth.

3. Spoon into demitasse cups or small dessert dishes. Press plastic wrap directly onto surface. Refrigerate several hours or until chilled. Garnish with whipped cream; sift cocoa over top, if desired.

Do not use instant pudding mix.

CHOCOLATE & CREAMY ORANGE MOUSSE

Makes 8 servings

$^1/_4$ cup ($^1/_2$ stick) butter or margarine

$^1/_4$ cup HERSHEY'S Cocoa

1 can (14 oz.) sweetened condensed milk (not evaporated milk), divided

2 tablespoons orange juice plus 2 teaspoons freshly grated orange peel OR 2 tablespoons orange-flavored liqueur, divided

2 cups (1 pt.) cold whipping cream

1. Melt butter in heavy saucepan over low heat; add cocoa, then $^2/_3$ cup sweetened condensed milk, stirring until smooth and slightly thickened. Pour mixture into medium bowl; cool to room temperature. Beat in 1 tablespoon orange juice and 1 teaspoon orange peel.

2. Beat whipping cream in large bowl until stiff. Fold half of whipped cream into chocolate mixture. In second medium bowl, stir together remaining sweetened condensed milk, remaining 1 tablespoon orange juice and 1 teaspoon orange peel. Fold in remaining whipped cream.

3. Spoon equal portions of chocolate mixture into 8 dessert dishes, making a depression in center of each. Spoon creamy orange mixture into center of each. Refrigerate until well chilled. Garnish as desired. Cover; refrigerate leftover dessert.

FIRESIDE STEAMED PUDDING

Makes 12 to 14 servings

1$^1/_2$ cups plain dry bread crumbs

1 cup sugar, divided

2 tablespoons all-purpose flour

$^1/_2$ teaspoon baking powder

$^1/_8$ teaspoon salt

6 eggs, separated

1 can (21 oz.) cherry pie filling, divided

2 tablespoons butter or margarine, melted

$^1/_2$ teaspoon almond extract

$^1/_4$ teaspoon red food color

1 cup HERSHEY'S MINICHIPS Semi-Sweet Chocolate

Cherry Whipped Cream (recipe follows)

1. Thoroughly grease 8-cup tube mold or heat-proof bowl.

2. Stir together bread crumbs, ¾ cup sugar, flour, baking powder and salt in large bowl. Stir together egg yolks, 1½ cups cherry pie filling, butter, almond extract and food color in medium bowl; add to crumb mixture, stirring gently until well blended.

3. Beat egg whites in another large bowl until foamy; gradually add remaining ¼ cup sugar, beating until stiff peaks form. Fold about ⅓ beaten whites into cherry mixture, blending thoroughly. Fold in remaining egg whites; gently fold in small chocolate chips. Pour batter into prepared tube mold. (If mold is open at top, cover opening with foil; grease top of foil.) Cover mold with wax paper and foil; tie securely with string.

4. Place a rack in a large kettle; pour water into kettle to top of rack. Heat water to boiling; place mold on rack. Cover kettle; steam over simmering water about 1½ hours or until wooden pick inserted comes out clean. (Additional water may be needed during steaming.) Remove from heat; cool in pan 5 minutes. Remove cover; unmold onto serving plate. Serve warm with Cherry Whipped Cream.

Cherry Whipped Cream: Beat 1 cup ($^1/_2$ pt.) cold whipping cream with $^1/_4$ cup powdered sugar in medium bowl until stiff; fold in pie filling remaining from pudding (about $^1/_2$ cup) and $^1/_2$ teaspoon almond extract.

CHOCOLATE SQUARES WITH NUTTY CARAMEL SAUCE

Makes 9 servings

- 1 cup sugar
- $3/4$ cup all-purpose flour
- $1/2$ cup HERSHEY'S Dutch Processed Cocoa or HERSHEY'S Cocoa
- $1/2$ teaspoon baking powder
- $1/2$ teaspoon salt
- $3/4$ cup vegetable oil
- $1/4$ cup milk
- 3 eggs
- $1/2$ teaspoon vanilla extract
- 1 bag (14 oz.) caramel candies
- $1/2$ cup water
- 1 cup pecan pieces
  Sweetened whipped cream (optional)

1. Heat oven to 350°F. Grease bottom only of 8-inch square baking pan.

2. Stir together sugar, flour, cocoa, baking powder and salt in medium bowl. Add oil, milk, eggs and vanilla; beat until smooth. Pour batter into prepared pan.

3. Bake 35 to 40 minutes or until wooden pick inserted in center comes out clean. Cool completely in pan on wire rack.

4. Remove wrappers from caramels. Combine caramels and water in small saucepan. Cook over low heat, stirring occasionally, until smooth and well blended. Stir in pecans; cool until thickened slightly. Cut cake into squares; serve with warm caramel nut sauce and sweetened whipped cream, if desired.

HERSHEY'S
RECIPE INDEX

HERSHEY'S
RECIPE INDEX

HERSHEY'S
RECIPE INDEX

HERSHEY'S
PRODUCT INDEX

HERSHEY'S

PRODUCT INDEX